Caroline Righton's

CREATE IT
— WITH —
PAPER
— IN AN —
EVENING

NEXUS SPECIAL INTERESTS

Caroline Righton's

CREATE IT
WITH
PAPER
IN AN
EVENING

DESIGNER
ELAINE DONOVAN
PHOTOGRAPHER
RICHARD LAING

NEXUS SPECIAL INTERESTS

Nexus Special Interests Ltd.
Nexus House
Boundary Way
Hemel Hempstead
Hertfordshire HP2 7ST
England

First published in Great Britain by Nexus Special Interests Ltd., 1998

ISBN 1-85486-175-1

Dedicated to Ben and James

Colour separations by PDQ, Bungay, Suffolk
Printed and bound in Great Britain by Jarrold Book Printing, Thetford, Norfolk

CONTENTS

INTRODUCTION

Life today can be so hectic that spare time is all the more precious and while it would be easy to spend that spare time catching up on the domestic chores or doing extra shopping I bet you wish you could just take a bit of time out for you occasionally and lose yourself in something absorbing and creative.

The trouble is, by the time you've got yourself organised to do anything productive it's time to stop again and you have to leave it half finished because of all the other demands on your time.

Well this book is for you. All the craft ideas in it are do-able in a few hours. Believe me, I've done them! If you add a call to your local craft store or artists' suppliers shop to your supermarket dash in the morning, then by the end of the same day you should have created something for yourself, your home or as a gift. More importantly you will have spent a lovely creative few hours which have relaxed you and certainly taken your mind off the million and one other things your children, partner or boss etc. want you to worry about.

Creating something in an evening with paper is easy. It seems to involve a bit of magic too because you really do seem to create something from nothing! If you want to do something uncomplicated and not too demanding have a go at papier mâché. If you want to do something that requires hardly any artistic talent but produces stunningly artistic results then découpage is for you, and finally if you don't mind a bit of water sloshing around and trying your hand at new techniques then make some hand-made paper.

PAPER

There are nine different projects in this book to do with paper and apart from drying time all of them are easily achievable in an evening.

PAPIER MACHE

I think all of us will have had a go at papier mâché when we were at school. I know that as soon as I started working on these projects the memories came flooding back of Henleaze Junior School in Bristol. At the very least you can make papier mâché items from just old newspapers and flour and water paste, things that most of us have at home. But by using other glues and a variety of techniques you will be able to make a durable attractive bowl for your home, a set of very individual earrings, or some napkin rings to complement your table setting.

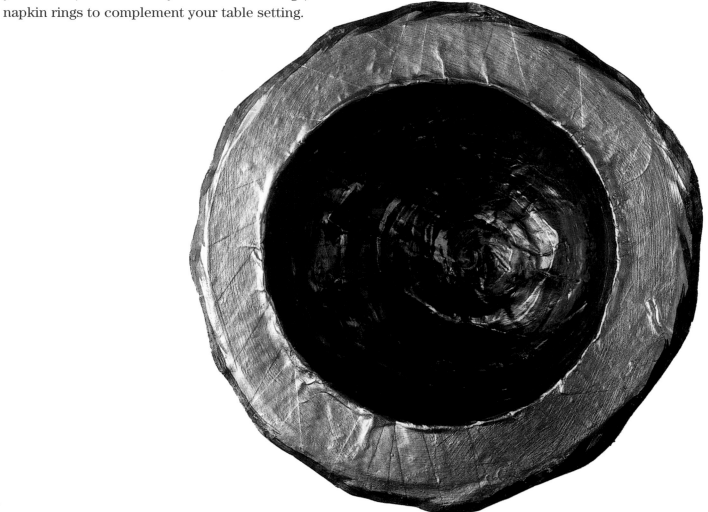

DECOUPAGE

Découpage is wonderful. It's almost impossible to believe that you can transform plain items into such things of beauty so quickly and with no need of great artistic ability. It's all about cutting out, sticking on and varnishing over! The box is straightforward découpage, the lamp shade is a little bit more fiddly - but not difficult - and the vase, well that's a cheat on a cheat as you don't even need to varnish it. It's incredibly quick to do and I hope you agree produces a stunning effect.

PAPER MAKING

When I first saw someone make some paper I couldn't believe it was SO simple. I had been a big fan of hand-made paper and over the years must have spent a fortune buying greetings cards or thank you notes made of hand-made paper with flowers pressed into them. It is messy - in that water goes everywhere - but that's not a problem if you have got plenty of newspaper. I do warn you however that it is addictive! I started off with greetings cards and then went on to make the notepaper with the pressed flowers and the scented lavender drawer liners all in one night.

PAPER
M A K I N G

There are three hand-made paper projects in this section of the book, however we all use so much paper in our lives that I'm sure you will be able to think of many other things to make once you have mastered the staggeringly simple method of making your own paper. I have spent a fortune buying hand-made paper greetings cards and notelets so I've included some ideas for those. The lavender drawer liners I often give as gifts and the pressed flower paper just had to be included because it's my personal favourite.

THE ORIGINS OF PAPER MAKING

The word 'paper' comes from the Greek word 'papuros' and we know that the ancient Greeks along with the ancient Romans and Egyptians made a sort of paper using the papyrus plant. They used to pound the stems of the plant until they were flat and then lay them out in criss-crossing layers covered by the waters of the River Nile before pressing the water out and leaving the sheet in the sun to dry.

This is really a far cry from paper-making today which is produced in great rolls by machinery but it's even further removed from hand-made paper-making today. It was the Chinese in approximately AD 105 who discovered the technique of making paper similar to our own. A significant part of their art and culture is the skill of calligraphy and they were motivated to find a better surface to write on than cloth or strips of wood or bamboo.

The Japanese turned the technique into a skilled craft and Japan's still the country most respected for its hand-made paper making. Peasant farmers work through the winter months using moulds made of paper and a flexible bamboo mesh to strain the water away.

The Japanese don't just make paper to write on - they use it almost as much as fabric. We have all seen the beautiful Japanese paper lanterns and umbrellas and fans, well in Japan they also use it for doors and windows. They actually make woven paper called 'shifu' by cutting a sheet of paper into strips, rolling these on a stone to make them into threads and then weaving these on a loom into cloth. This cloth is then cut and sewn to make kimonos, jackets and purses. Just as earlier we heard how Oriental warriors made hardened papier mâché helmets - so the Japanese made lightweight armour from paper mixed with other materials.

Until approximately 200 years ago all paper in the Western world was made by hand, mainly from fabric. The paper mills bought cast-off clothing, collected by rag and bone men who toured the streets with their carts.

At this point of course paper was still being made one sheet at a time. At the papermills the rags would be soaked and pulverised and then a 'vat man' would dip a large mould strainer into a vat of 'pulp stock'. Then another workman would 'couch' or press the wet sheet while it was on the mould and finally a third worker in the team would separate the sheets from the mould and place them under a corkscrew type clamp press.

Once machinery to make paper was invented in the late eighteenth century there just wasn't enough material to make the paper to meet demand. Machine-made paper was cheaper and the manufacturers hit on pulping wood and in particular the fibres from conifer trees.

Apparently they got this idea from studying the way wasps chew old wood to make sawdust which they then mix with their saliva to make pulp paper nests to lay their eggs in.

Today because the world is using up paper faster than trees can be grown to produce it there is a great movement towards recycling. Reviving the tradition of making hand-made paper is one way we can do our bit!

Mesh

Liquidizer

Paper

Plant matter

Trays

Scissors

Mounting cards

Kitchen cloth

Dried pot pourri

Aromatic essence

Pressed flowers

Glue

Water

EQUIPMENT

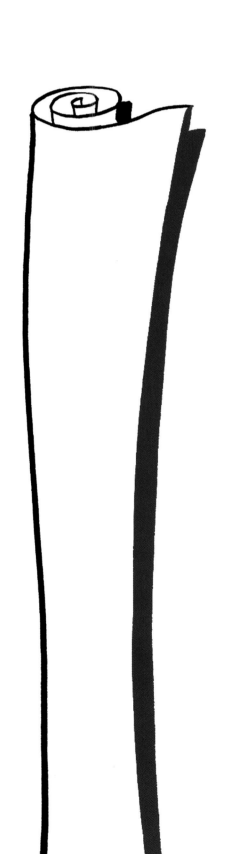

You can buy special sieves to make paper. However I find that a straightforward piece of fine **mesh** does the job perfectly and the sort I use can be bought really cheaply from car and bike accessory shops where it is used to fill the bodywork of vehicles. It is so fine you can cut shapes with sharp scissors. You will need loads of old **newspapers** to mop up the water that you press out of your paper and some **kitchen cloth** such as J-cloths to blot the pulp onto. Virtually any **paper**, coloured or plain, can be recycled and you can also make pulp from plant matter too, such as onion skins, cabbage leaves and pineapple tops.

You need to soak it in a bowl and pulverise it, a **liquidizer** will make quick work of this. Once you have made your pulp you can add all manner of coloured paints or other objects to it such as **pot pourri**, **aromatic essences** or **seeds** before making the paper or you can position **pressed flowers** into the wet sheets before they dry. If you are making pictures or cards to send you will of course need **mounting card** and **glue**.

Making paper fulfils several things for me. At the end of a making session when I have several sheets of sodden pulp drying out I know that I have made some really individual items. They are going to give added value and meaning to those I give them to as greetings and thank-you cards. But there is also the satisfaction of recycling paper and very quickly making something, virtually out of nothing, for free.

TECHNIQUES

Believe it or not I have actually made paper from the vegetable peelings of Sunday lunch. I couldn't find a use for it, but it did prove the point to a disbelieving friend that you can make paper from virtually any plant or vegetable matter. Onions are particularly good.

Plants with stringy stalks such as celery, bamboo, rhubarb, sunflowers, corn on the cob or plants with long leaves such as reeds, rushes, pampas grass and irises are all really good.

It is slightly more complicated to make paper from plant matter because you have to really break down the raw material to release the fibres. You do this by chopping or shredding it all up into small pieces, covering it with water in a pan, bringing it to the boil and then letting it simmer for about an hour. Strain it and then thoroughly rinse it under a running tap until the water runs clear. If you don't like the colour you can leave it to soak in diluted bleach for an hour to lighten the colour and then rinse it well. You then proceed to make your pulp in the same way as for recycled paper although at the drying stage you may want to place the paper under weights as plant matter paper is subject to some shrinkage.

Different colour papers can be achieved by either using different colour papers to make your pulp or by adding paints to the pulp. You could mix coloured pulps to get interesting effects. Another way of colouring your paper is with natural dyes. Back to the onion skins, the boiled water from them would give a plain white pulp a beige colour. Try curry powder and camomile tea for yellow and herbal teas for an interesting grey!

You can also scent your paper with herbs and aromatic essences. Either mix dried flowers, petals or stalks into the pulp or scatter them onto the wet pressed out paper sheets. I prefer the latter technique because you have a little more control. Sprinkle a few drops of aromatic essence onto the dried paper. My favourite herb is lavender and lavender oil with the pressed flowers gives a lovely effect but I have also used rosemary and lemon balm.

You can also add larger pressed flowers such as cornflower florets or rose petals or even bits of ribbon or tinsel to the final stage of paper making. It's easier though to just fix pressed flowers to the dried paper with a small dab of glue.

Always remember that you will need to treat or 'size' your hand-made paper if you intend to write on it. Mix one fifth of a teaspoon full of cold water laundry starch with a little water and mix into the pulp. A tablespoonful of PVA glue mixed in a jar of water will do the same trick.

STEP-BY-STEP

To make straightforward hand-made paper you can use almost any kind of paper for recycling that has not got a shiny surface although newsprint will make a dingy shade of paper and won't be terribly strong.

PREPARE YOUR PAPER

Treat each colour separately. The quickest way is using a liquidizer. Put a handful of torn paper into the liquidizer and fill it two thirds full with water and pulse liquidize for up to 30 seconds. If you are doing it by hand tear the paper into small pieces and soak before whisking the pieces around to make a mushy pulp.

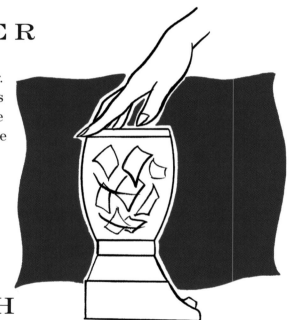

PREPARE YOUR MESH

Pour the pulp into a tray larger than your mesh or sieve and top up with water.

If you are using the fine mesh you can cut shapes out such as hearts and diamonds although I suggest you start with a rectangle of approximately 7cm by 15cm.

Water, water, everywhere is what happens with paper making so spread your work surface with newspaper and put one thick pile on the right of the table (if you are right-handed). Place the kitchen cloth, folded widthways, on top of this thick pile.

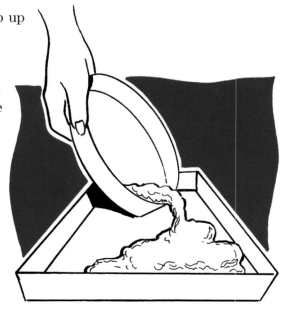

LIFTING THE PULP

Give the pulp a stir with your fingers so there is plenty of pulp floating on the surface and then take the piece of mesh or the sieve and slip it into the pulp at an angle. Straighten it so it is effectively submerged below the surface with plenty of pulp floating on top. Holding it very carefully by the edges lift it out and let the water drain through leaving just pulp.

PRESSING THE PULP

Lift over to the kitchen cloth on the pile of newspaper and in one gentle movement flip it pulp side down and press lightly on top with the palm of your hand.

PEELING THE MESH

Then carefully pick at one corner of the mesh so that it lifts free of the pulp, which should be sticking to the cloth and peel the mesh away.
You have made your first piece of paper.

Repeat the process, placing pieces so they slightly overlap to build up as large an area as you want. Leave it to dry on a flat surface and then the kitchen cloth should peel away easily.

If you want your paper extra flat either roll over it with a rolling pin when it is still a bit damp or leave it to dry under a board and weights. Personally I prefer the more textured appearance.

PAPER FROM PLANTS

YOU WILL NEED

The outer skins of a large onion

A saucepan

Water

Some white paper for recycling

A sieve

Tray for pulp

Mesh

PVA glue

A liquidizer

Newspaper

Kitchen cloth

Pressed flowers

I mixed paper and plant matter pulp to get this interesting effect.

PAPER FROM PLANTS

Perfect for 'sob stories'! Writing paper made from onion skins and no....it doesn't smell!

SCENTED DRAWER LINERS

YOU WILL NEED

White paper

Water

Tray for pulp

Liquidizer

Mesh

3 Kitchen cloths

Newspaper

Lavender

Lavender oil

Spread yourself out for this project so that you can make your sheets of paper the same size as your drawers. Straighten the edges by pushing the pulp in with a knife while it is wet.

SCENTED DRAWER LINERS

This perfect present is full of scent and texture making an attractive drawer liner.

CARDS

YOU WILL NEED

Different coloured papers for recycling or

Paints

Water

Liquidizer

Trays

Fine mesh

Scissors

Newspaper

Kitchen cloths

Scraps of ribbon or tinsel

PVA glue

Gold or silver pens

Glue

Mounting card

Start by making your basic rectangle and then add shapes on top and define or embellish with pens or decoration when dry. Don't despair of achieving a good effect, wait until your creations have dried - they will always look much better then!

A card to say thank you or happy birthday will have extra special meaning if you have made it yourself. Experiment and develop your own distinctive style!

WHY STOP THERE?

Think how many times you use paper during the course of the day and now think what you can make with your new skill. Here are some ideas.

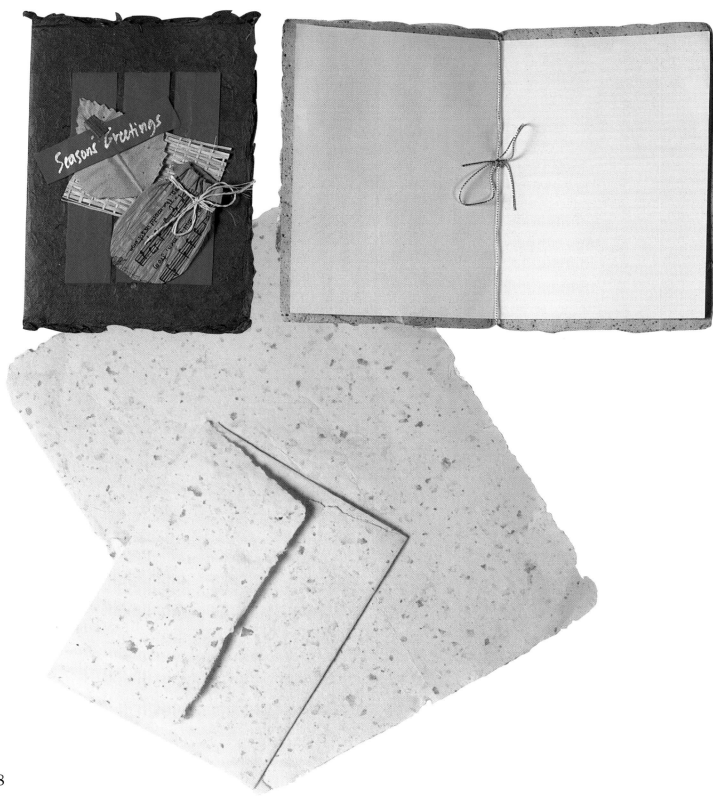

DECOUPAGE

Découpage is one of my favourite crafts and if you haven't ever tried it I have to warn you that you could become seriously hooked! It's a craft that can easily be done in an evening and you will see how simple it is to transform the plainest object into a thing of beauty within a couple of hours. However, découpage can also become a full-time hobby and before you know it you will find yourself saving odd bits of wrapping paper and cutting out designs in quiet moments ahead of when you want to actually start a découpage project.

31

THE ORIGINS OF DECOUPAGE

Découpage has a long and complicated history because it is really an amalgamation of several different crafts. It has been influenced by the paper cutting of the ancient Chinese, the felt appliqué work of Siberia and the painted paper cut-out craft of Polish folk art.

The word is French, meaning 'cutting out' and it is quite simply the art of cutting and pasting cut-outs to simulate painting on wood, metal or glass surfaces.

As we know it, découpage originated in France in the seventeenth century as furniture decoration. It was terribly fashionable to have Chinese painted and lacquered furniture.

But the imports couldn't keep up with the demand and so French craftsmen found that they could achieve much the same effect by varnishing over pre-painted and printed designs so that the picture was completely submerged by the varnish and gave the impression of being hand-painted. Craftsmen in other parts of Europe were also working along the same lines and it soon spread through the continent and by the eighteenth century it had become a fashionable hobby in the main European courts.

Sheets of pictures were printed expressly for the purpose of découpage and it became a favourite pursuit of aristocratic women, who would sit cutting out the designs to apply them to fans, screens and toilet articles such as hairbrushes

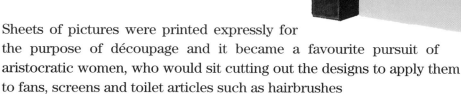

It was all the rage particularly in the French court during the 1780s. While one can conjure up the picture of Marie Antoinette and her girlfriends cutting out pretty pictures while nibbling their cake, it's not so easy to visualise them painting on coat after coat of varnish to get a perfect finish. Methinks it was the enjoyment of the craft as a hobby rather than the skill that appealed to them.

It found favour in Britain during the Victorian era when again especially produced pre-printed designs were cut out by genteel, fashionable ladies and stuck onto all manner of items. The big speciality of the time was to decorate a screen with these patterns and designs, which they called 'scraps'.

Another form of découpage called potichomanie became popular in the late eighteenth century. This process involved covering the inside surface of a glass vase with cut-out paper designs and pictures to give the impression of decorated porcelain.

The 1920s saw découpage again become fashionable with the advent of Art Deco and the Parisian designer Jean Michel Frank used it to decorate his famous Parsons tables. And from the 1960s to today the craft has enjoyed a steady following and recognition as an achievable hobby for those who want to decorate items for their home.

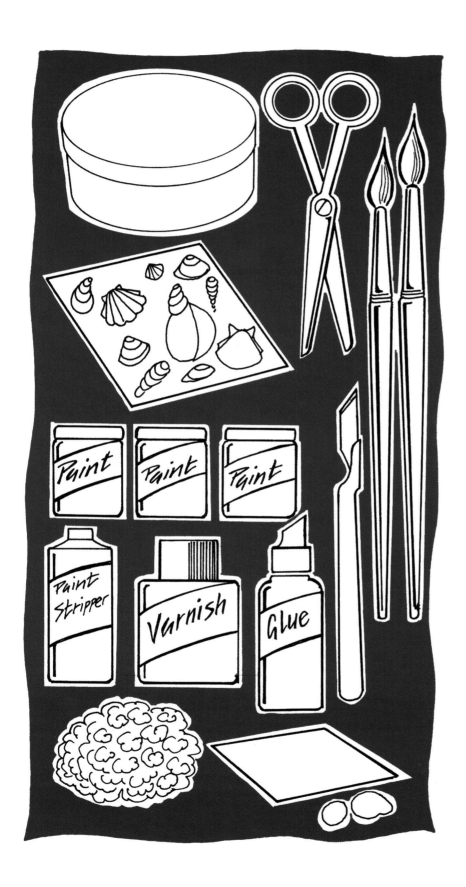

A blank item

Cut-outs

Brushes

Glue

Paints

Paint stripper

Sandpaper

Wire wool

Scissors or scalpel

Varnish

Blu-Tack

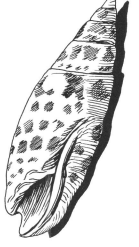

EQUIPMENT

Practically anything can be découpage so you don't need to buy a **blank item** to decorate. Instead look around your home or browse in local junk shops or car boot sales to find something with a good basic shape that you can embellish.

That said, however, unless you buy a prepared blank item you are going to have to spend some time preparing the surface. More about this in the step-by-step instructions.

Good pictures for your **cut-outs** can be found everywhere. You can buy découpage resource books but wrapping paper is good, so too are old books and calendars. Be imaginative and experiment with enlarging maps, sheet music or calligraphy. **Blu-Tack** is useful to stick them on upright items to experiment with the positioning.

Use the best **brushes** you can afford - there is nothing more infuriating than having to keep picking loose hairs out of your **varnish** - or even worse to spot one stuck solid when the finished item is dry.

I'm a big fan of **PVA glue** although there are lots of others on the market including the spray adhesives.

Choose quick-drying craft **paints** suitable for going on your blank item. If you are not using a pre-bought blank you will need to prime and undercoat.

And of course you will have needed to strip and rub down your blank item with **wire wool** and **sandpaper** if it's a junk shop find to make sure the surface is smooth and grease-free before you paint. Very fine sandpaper can be useful too if you want to apply lots of layers of varnish for lightly rubbing down between coats. Very sharp scissors will make cutting out easy and a scalpel can be useful.

The moment you start applying the varnish is the moment the découpage magic starts so use either a good polyurethane or acrylic **varnish** and make sure it's quick drying. You can also buy special crackle glaze finishes to give an antique look to your work.

Well you can't say I haven't warned you. You are about to take up a craft which will mean that never again will you be able to look at a blank, plain object without seeing the potential for wonderful decoration with découpage.

TECHNIQUES

Because découpage is quite simply the art of cutting out, sticking on and then varnishing over to submerge the design all the techniques are variations on the basic method

Monochrome découpage can look really effective. Experiment with enlarging prints on a photocopier. Use larger sheets of text, music or maps as a background for other smaller cut-outs.

If you put a teabag into hot water and then squeeze it out you can gently wipe it over your black and white surface to get an instant 'old' effect.

If you are going for the antique look then try the crackle varnishes that are available from most craft shops and artists' suppliers. It is a two-stage process that usually involves painting a fast-drying varnish over the surface. Then you can also rub in and wipe off a tint or liquid wax to really get the antique effect.

The potichomanie technique is where cut-outs are stuck on the inside of a glass object. No varnish is used but the cut-outs and the inside of the glass are painted. Make sure you can get your hands inside your chosen object. Position your cut-outs with bits of Blu-Tack on the outside, then coating the right side of the designs with glue, one-by-one carefully stick them in position on the inside. When the glue has dried and any surplus has been removed make sure the inside is completely clean and dry and then paint the inside over the paper cut-outs with short spiralling outwards brush strokes.

You can also use fabric designs for your cut-outs. This is particularly effective if you want to decorate wicker furniture or baskets. Be generous with the glue and really press the cut-out well into the weave of the wicker with a cloth that has been wrung out in hot water. You are likely to need to use a heavier duty varnish and give the item at least three coats.

STEP-BY-STEP

Preparation is the watchword of découpage. Make sure you have everything you need at the outset. If you plan to decorate an old item you must strip off any old paint or varnish, fill any holes or cracks with wood filler or use rust remover and wire wool to get a smooth surface.

Assuming you are tackling a straightforward découpage technique, first paint over your blank item with a base coat. Make sure your brush strokes are all in the same direction. Check for drips and leave to dry. Apply a second coat.

While it is drying cut out your chosen pictures. Protect your work surface and whenever possible move the paper rather than the scalpel. Cut very neatly around all the shapes and place them on the item, experimenting until you are completely happy. I use tiny pieces of Blu-Tack if it's an upright item.

When you are happy with the end arrangement put a small amount of glue on the back of each paper cut-out and stick in place, making sure it is absolutely smooth and all edges are well stuck down. Carefully wipe off any excess glue that might ooze out.

Once the cut-outs are stuck down you could add more paint or colour around the pictures and pattern.

When your item is completely dry you can start applying varnish. It's entirely up to you how many coats you put on. The first item of découpage I made only had two layers and I was very happy and pleased with the result.

Most importantly apply the varnish in generous brush strokes, brushing it out lightly across the surface and again avoid drips and runs at all costs. Leave to dry before putting on additional coats.

LAMPSHADE

YOU WILL NEED

A cheap plain white lampshade

A sheet of music enlarged on a photocopier (4 copies)

Photocopies of line drawings of musical instruments

A teabag

Scissors

PVA glue

Brush for glue

Black paint

Brush for paint

Varnish

Brush for varnish

You can get the shape of your lampshade by rolling the top rim carefully around on a sheet of newspaper to make a template. As you roll hold a pen to mark its track onto the newspaper. Do the same with the bottom rim. Cut out this template, stick together enough sheet music to cover the pattern area and cut out, leaving a small overlap for the seam. Mop over with a wet teabag and then leave to dry before sticking it onto the lampshade. Decorate with the cut-out line drawings, also given the teabag treatment, put a black line as edging and you are ready to start varnishing.

LAMPSHADE

I was really thrilled when I made this in just a couple of hours. It was an instant success judging by the number of comments people made about it. I first saw sheet music used in decoupage on *The Craft Show* with craftswoman Juliet Bawden who also crackle-glazed a CD holder which looked fantastic.

KEEPSAKE BOX

YOU WILL NEED

A blank box

Paints

Brushes for paints

Cut-outs

Scissors

PVA glue

Brush for glue

Varnish

Brush for varnish

I've lightly brushed gold paint over cream around the cut-outs on this box after sticking them on but before varnishing to give a soft shimmery pastel hue.

KEEPSAKE BOX

A special box for keepsakes. Love letters, photos of children or even memorabilia such as invitations or theatre programmes can be kept in a box as special as its contents.

POTICHOMANIE VASE

YOU WILL NEED

Paper cut-outs

Blu-Tack

PVA glue

A brush for the glue

Paints - oil-based eggshell is good

A brush for the paint.

Make sure the vase is big enough to get your hand inside and work with a small amount of paint on your brush to prevent runs and dribbles.

POTICHOMANIE VASE

Never mind making this in an evening - I finished this in an hour!

WHY STOP THERE!

Talk about makeover magic! Découpage will turn any sow's ear of an item into a silken purse in just a few hours....

PAPIER
M A C H E

I hope the three papier mâché projects in this book are different enough to give you a choice of techniques and designs to inspire you to create an object for yourself or for your home. The simplest project is probably the napkin rings and they are a great and quick way to personalise or theme your dinner table. The bowl incorporates both layering and pulp paper if you want to try your hand at both. You will have to wait for the layering to dry before you add the pulp, which will make it stronger but isn't essential. The jewellery is very quick to make - the originality is in the way you choose to decorate the items.

THE ORIGINS OF PAPIER MACHE

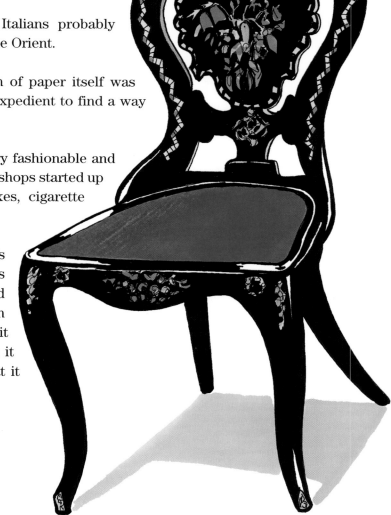

You could be forgiven for thinking that papier mâché must be a craft with French origins. Well it's not. The term 'papier mâché' was only coined by immigrant French workers who were working in London in the eighteenth century. They were working for a manufacturer of items made of 'chewed paper' - ' mâché ' means 'to chew.' I find it hard to believe but there are accounts of people actually chewing paper into pulp before it was mashed by machines.

The method of producing objects from moulded pulped paper has been known from ancient times in the Orient. There are records of papier mâché being used to make war helmets for the Chinese which they coated with lacquer to harden them.

Then the craft spread to Europe with the Italians probably learning it via the Venetian Trade Route from the Orient.

We shouldn't forget that the actual production of paper itself was relatively new and so it was considered most expedient to find a way to recycle it.

Lacquering, painting and japanning became very fashionable and Russian, French and English factories and workshops started up in the seventeenth century making snuff boxes, cigarette cases, trays and chests of various sorts.

Techniques really are little different to today's methods. Robert Boyle (1627 - 1691) wrote in his book *Uses of Natural Things* that one should take slips of brown paper and "boil them in Common Water and mash it with a stick while it boils. When it has almost become a paste, take it from the water and put it in a mortar and beat it well until it is reduced to a pulp".

The eighteenth century saw the craft go from strength to strength with wonderful architectural fittings being made with sawdust being added to the paper pulp for strength.

All the glorious gilded wall brackets, sconces and decorative plaques of this time are likely to have been made from papier mâché. It was finding favour in America too and it's recorded that George Washington ordered papier mâché ceiling 'ornaments' from London - while his wife Martha expressed an interest in having papier mâché decoration added to her curtain poles.

Into the nineteenth century and the uses and decoration of papier mâché pieces became more and more ornate. Lap desks, clock cases, and casings for the newly invented daguerreotypes, which was the forerunner to the camera, were ornamented in gold leaf and pearl shell.

It became very fashionable to seek unusual sources of paper to recycle and one instance records how an Act of Congress in America in 1874 allowed retired banknotes to be pulped and mixed with soda, ash and lime which destroyed their identity. This was used to make busts of prominent Americans and replicas of national monuments.

Today papier mâché is a popular material to make objects, jewellery, theatrical masks and props as well as newspaper logs for fire kindling.

But perhaps the most enduring use of papier mâché should be attributed to the schoolboy's carefully chewed paper bullet, otherwise known as a spitball which is the nearest we get today to the old English chewed paper!

Bowl

Sieve

Liquidizer

Cocktail sticks or darning needle

Scissors

Paint brushes

Petroleum jelly

Paper

Gesso

Paints

Glue

Balloons

Cardboard tubing

Varnish

EQUIPMENT

The equipment you need to make items from papier mâché is about as basic as you can get..

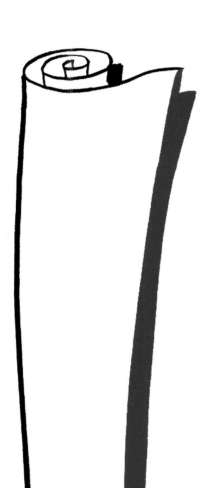

Bowl: well several actually, of varying sizes to soak your paper and to mix up your glue etc.

Sieve: this is really useful to shake out all the excess water so you are left with a wonderfully smooth pulp.

Liquidizer: it's a lot easier to mash the soaked paper with one - otherwise use fingers and a fork.

Cocktail sticks or **darning needle:** to make holes in while it's still soft.

Scissors: to trim rims and cut card bases.

Paint brushes: various sizes for glues, paints and varnishes.

Petroleum jelly: this is essential if you use anything other than a balloon as your mould.

Paper: just about any sort apart from highly glossed. Newsprint is excellent. Coloured cartridge paper will give you coloured pulp.

Gesso: or emulsion paint to prime the dried article so you can paint it.

Paints: any sort that are suitable for paper and quick drying.

Glue: wallpaper paste works although I like PVA glue best .

Balloons: good quality ones.

Cardboard tubing: inside of kitchen rolls etc.

Varnish: a quick-drying clear gloss is best.

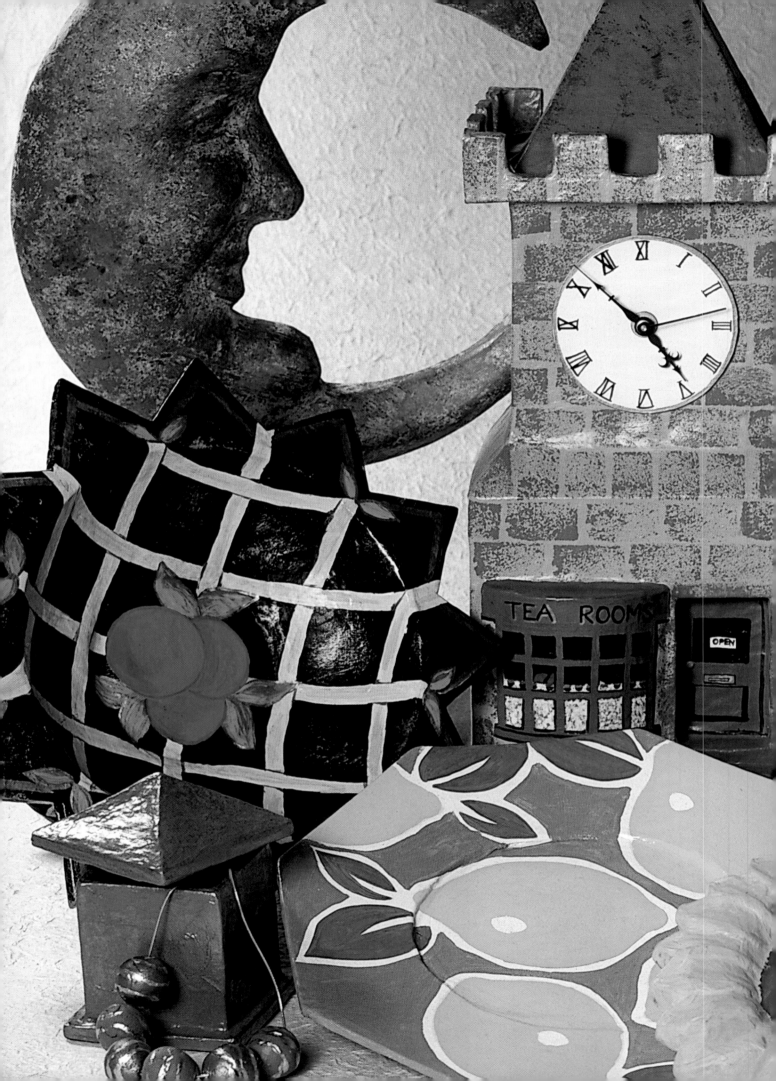

I think most adults who decide to have a go at papier mâché are irresistibly drawn to blowing up a balloon and making a bowl shape but you can be much more ambitious. Papier mâché is a very versatile craft and in fact lends itself to being moulded into just about any shape, wrapped around almost any mould and then decorated and turned into any number of useful or beautiful items.

TECHNIQUES

The basic techniques of layering paper and making pulp papier mâché are explained in the step-by-step instructions. I recommend that whatever technique you try begin using newsprint - my personal favourite is the *Financial Times*. Here I explain a few other tricks in both making your basic item and then decorating it.

SOLID MOULDS

If you want to mould your papier mâché around something other than a balloon, such as a bowl perhaps, then make sure you smear it well first with petroleum jelly so the dried shape will lift off easily.

USING TEMPLATES

You can wrap strips of gluey paper around other shapes that will remain hidden inside the crafted item. I can remember making structures with chicken wire as a child. But cutting up thick cardboard boxes and making templates which you then cover with pulp is another good way to build up an interesting shape on a sturdy base. Also if you use a coloured base pulp there'll be less painting to do later.

RIMS, HANDLES AND BASES

Thick cardboard is also really good for adding rims, handles and bases. Cut out the shapes you want and then stick them onto your item using tape, and then just wrap more paper strips around them to cover the joins or push bits of paper pulp into the gaps.

Don't feel trapped by using just one method. My most effective creations have been where I've applied pulp on top of layered papier mâché that I've moulded around a balloon, added some trims and then applied a few more layers to get a smoother effect. Needless to say you won't finish a project like that in an evening!

PULP MIXTURES

Also what about mixing things in with the pulp you use to make your items? Dried flowers perhaps in a bowl that is going to be used to hold pot pourri or cut up tinsel in decorative bowls for Christmas. Once you've got your basic shape made and dried there is virtually no limit to the way you can decorate it.

DECORATION

After priming with either gesso or emulsion paint you can, of course, simply paint it and varnish it or you could stick on beads, use fake gold leaf to gild it or add pieces of torn paper and other items to make a collage effect.

One clever trick is to build up a relief pattern on your item with either coiled rope or twine, or even use the wall filler that comes in a tube and is used in DIY.

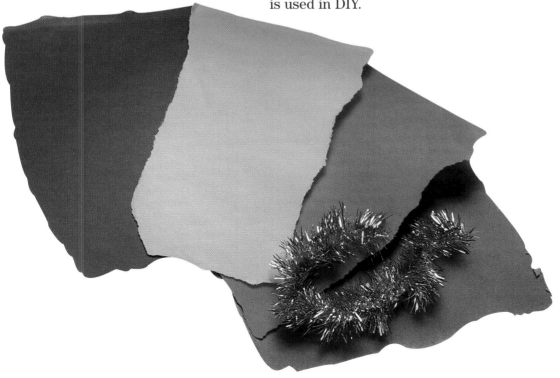

STEP-BY-STEP

The first thing to do is to put the kettle on and make a cup of tea or coffee! You'll get quite sticky making papier mâché and it's as well to think ahead to essentials like the drink you'll want along the way!

Gather all the things you will need to make your item. Prepare your mould or base template, for example, blow up your balloon, trim the cardboard tubing, cut out your template.

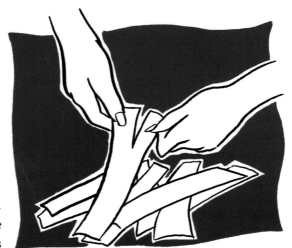

If you are working with a balloon place it upside down in a china or glass bowl to hold it steady. If you plan to use the layering technique tear up the newspaper into strips approximately 5cm by 14cm.

Brush both sides of the paper with glue for the first layer and place on the balloon, mould or template overlapping the pieces of paper as you work. Do four layers. Leave to dry.

If you want to add a base, rim or handles cut these out of thick cardboard or stiff card and stick on with tape and then cover the joins with more layered sticky paper. Leave in a warm place to dry before decorating.

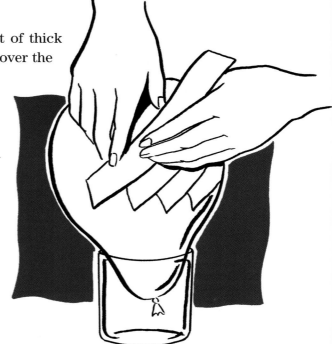

When it feels dry, pop the balloon or remove the mould. Now you can paint over with fast-drying gesso or emulsion and get decorating your item.

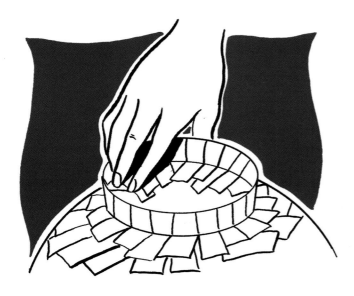

To make pulp papier mâché is very easy and quick if you have a liquidizer. Put a handful of torn paper into it and then fill it two-thirds full with water and pulse liquidize for 15 seconds. If you haven't got a liquidizer tear the paper up into postage stamp-sized pieces, place in a bowl and cover with warm water to soak for a couple of hours before tipping out half the water and mashing the paper to a mushy pulp using a fork or whisk.

Pour the watery pulp through a sieve shaking it until you have a soft mixture that's not too wet and can be moulded and formed into shapes. Add some glue bit by bit, mixing it with your hands until it resembles soft clay and then, working with a little at a time, push it onto your mould, making sure there are no gaps. Leave to dry.

Paint over with gesso or white emulsion to give a good primed surface to decorate.

A BOWL

YOU WILL NEED

A large good quality balloon

Paper - one section of the Financial Times or any other broadsheet should be enough

PVA glue

Stiff card

Tape

Scissors

Gesso or white emulsion

Paints

Brushes for glue, paint and varnish

Varnish

A balloon mould was used to make this bowl with layered papier mâché. A rim has been added and then I've freehand painted it with wonderful swirling blues, purples and metallic colours before varnishing.
You could add a layer of pulped papier mâché around the outside when the layers have dried and then paint that another colour and roughly brush gold or silver over it to give a gilded effect. The pulp would add interest and make the bowl stronger and the metallic brushing would make a feature of the different texture!

A BOWL

Go on! Get blowing up that balloon and relive a few childhood memories. This time though you'll end up with a beautiful bowl for your home rather than marks out of ten!

NAPKIN RINGS

YOU WILL NEED

Stiff cardboard tube

Paper

Gesso

Paints

Varnish

Brushes

You won't need too many layers of paper wrapped around your tubes to disguise their humble beginnings.

NAPKIN RINGS

I decorated these napkin rings with burgundy, green and gold paints to complement my table linen and crockery.

EARRINGS, NECKLACE AND PENDANT

YOU WILL NEED

Paper

Card

PVA glue

Gesso or white emulsion

Jewellery fastenings

Paints

Darning needle or cocktail stick

Varnish

Brushes for glue

Paint and varnish

Make beads out of pulp or layer strips of paper around a thick card shape to make jewellery. Remember to poke a hole through with a thick needle or cocktail stick while the paper is still damp.

EARRINGS, NECKLACE AND PENDANT

Jewel colours and dramatic black and gold paints disguise this jewellery's humble origins.

WHY STOP THERE?

Just a few other papier mâché ideas - start saving paper now...

KITS

I have developed a range of kits complementary to this book. Each kit contains everything you will need and at the end you should have enjoyed creating a beautiful item.

Paper Making: Paper is such a functional item that there is something quite compelling about recycling and making your own hand-made paper which can in itself be beautiful and interesting.

Contents:
- Trays
- Mesh
- Dried Lavender
- Lavender Essence/Oil
- Pressed Flowers
- Cartridge Paper
- Recycled White Paper
- White Card
- Scissors
- Cloth

Découpage: This is one of my favourite crafts. It is one of the simplest and most effective ways of completely and easily transforming everyday objects into items of beauty. This box is attractive and useful and makes a good introduction to the craft.

Contents:
- Scalpel
- Varnish
- Paints
- Découpage Paper Sheets
- Brushes
- PVA Glue
- Blank Box

Papier Mâché: Today, decorative papier mâché items can cost a fortune in the shops. This is something that most of us first did at school. When you start mixing the paste and pulping the paper to make this colourful gold and varnished bowl, the memories will come flooding back.

Contents:
- Gesso
- Paste
- Paints
- Paper
- Card
- Balloon
- Brushes
- Varnish

All the above are available from all good craft stores and by mail order from:

Really Vital Productions Ltd
PO Box 330
Slough SL2 3FH
Telephone orders call the orderline on 01753 648780

INDEX

EQUIPMENT AND SUPPLIERS

It wasn't so long ago that anyone interested in craft had to scour the back of specialist magazines to find the mail order outlets that stocked the materials and components needed. Either that or you hoped that the local haberdashery department or artists' materials shop might have it in stock.

Things are very different today. While many high street shops now stock craft materials, we've also got several large craft shop chains both in town centres and in out of town shopping malls. These massive 'sheds' have got very extensive ranges of stock and are also extremely competitive pricewise which is good news for the shopper.

I'm a great browser and often set off to buy a couple of small items only to return home with the essentials to start a whole new craft.

New products are being developed all the time to make craft easier, from new paints and clays to bigger and more imaginative ranges of blanks to decorate and embellish.

Alongside all the products you will often find details of courses and workshops in your locality and one thing that seems to be universal to all suppliers, from the local art shop, to the mail-order girl on the end of the phone to the person on the check-out till in the craft 'shed' is a shared enthusiasm to help you and me get the most out of our craft.

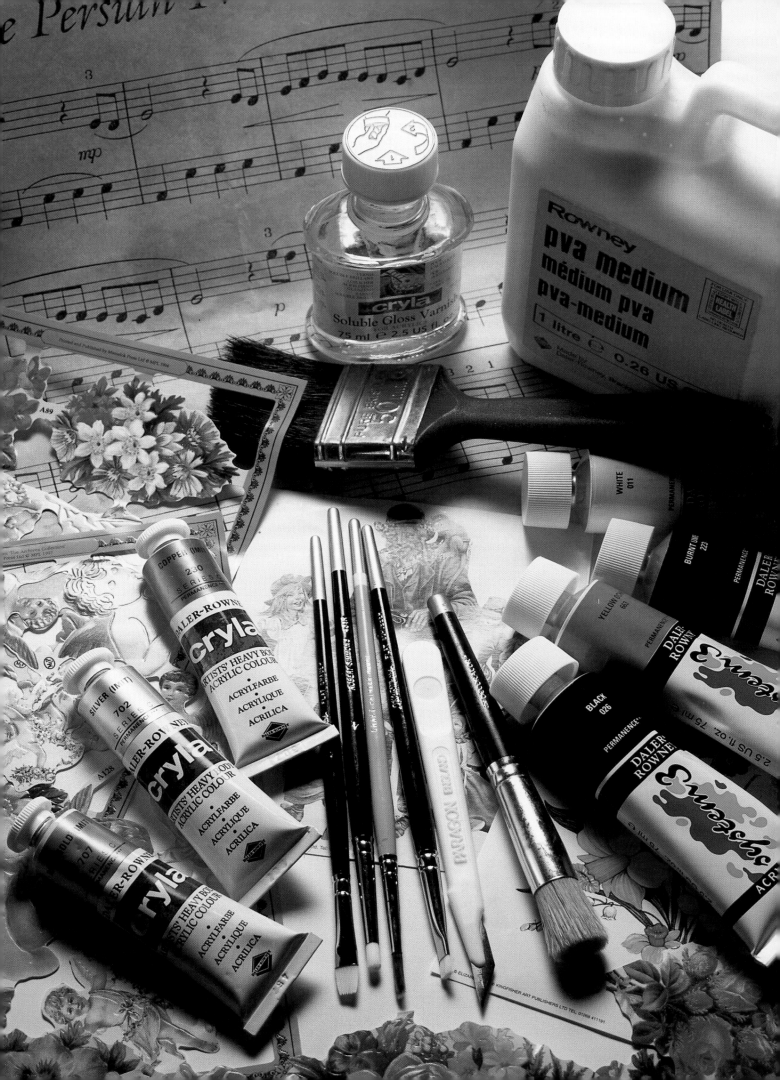

SUPPLIERS

Manufacturers, Importers and Wholesalers

Atlascraft
4 Plumtree St
The Lace Market
Nottingham
NG1 1JL
For your local suppliers please call customer services :
Tel: 0115 9415280
Fax: 0115 9415281

*A wide range of products covering most crafts. Main importers of Deka paints.
Their range is available at John Lewis Partnership Shops
and on Mail Order from:*

Cats Group
PO Box 12
Saxmundham
Suffolk
Tel: 01728 648717

ColArt Fine Art & Graphics Ltd
Whitefriars Avenue
Harrow
Middlesex
HA3 5RH
For your local suppliers please call customer services:
Tel: 0181 427 4343
Fax: 0181 863 7177

*A large portfolio of well-known branded fine art materials including Winsor &
Newton, Lefranc & Bourgeois and Dryad.*

Daler Rowney Ltd
P.O.Box 10
Bracknell
Berkshire
RG12 8ST
For your local suppliers please call customer services :
Tel: 01344 424621
Fax: 01344 486511

*Largest manufacturer of a fully comprehensive range of colours, brushes, surfaces
and artists and craft accessories*

Philip & Tacey Ltd
North Way
Andover
Hampshire
SP10 5BA
For your local suppliers please call customer services :
Tel: 01264 332171
Fax: 01264 332226
E-Mail: sales@philipandtacey.co.uk

*One of the longest established family firms in the arts and craft business. They carry
a large range of stock and are the importers of the well-known Pebeo range of paints.*

SUPPLIERS

Retail, Mail Order and Training Workshops

Creative World
The Bishop Centre
Bath Rd, Taplow
Berkshire SL6 0NY
Tel: 01628 661331
and at

Creative World
The Galleries
Bristol
Tel: 0117 929 7775

These are one of the new expanding chains of larger shops. They carry thousands of lines covering all crafts. Good for browsing!

Mulberry Craft
Cherry Tree House
7 Dean St
Marlow, Bucks
Tel: 01628 487900
Fax: 01628 475810
E-Mail: Mulberrycraft@BTInternet.com

Retail workshop and mail order. Offer an extensive range of supplies both retail and mail order. Chris Thompson and her team are always willing to give friendly advice and also offer training courses and workshops .

Kingfisher Ltd
Unit One
Christy Court
Southfields
Basildon, Essex
SS15 6TL
Tel: 01268 411191

A printer by trade but also have a varied range of découpage cut outs.

Ginger Gallery
84/86 Hotwells Road
Bristol BS8 4UB
Tel: 01179 292527

A lovely little gallery showing contemporary jewelry, ceramics, painting, sculpture and if you want to see how its really done a lovely display of papier mâché by Stephanie Chown. Expert classes for beginners.

Jacksons Mail Order
2 Victoria Avenue
Great Sankey
Warrington WA5 3NA
Tel/Fax: 01925 722223

Découpage specialists. A full mail order service including 3D découpage.

Nexus presents "Create It .....In an Evening", a series of books developed by Caroline Righton (your regular columnist on *Popular Crafts* TV presenter, producer, journalist and craft specialist), in response to the growing demand for innovative craft books suitable for today's busy lifestyle.

Other titles in this series

If you have enjoyed making the projects in this book, why not try your hand at other crafts? Other titles in this series include:

Create it with Paint in an Evening — Nine projects for painting on silk, glass or fabric. All are easily achievable by beginners with simple illustrated instructions and full colour throughout.

ISBN 1-85486-174-3

Create it with Wax, Clay & Plaster in an Evening — Another nine easy-to make projects using wax, clay and plaster. Again split into three sections each one comprising an introduction, equipment list, techniques and a step-by-step guide to the basic skills needed.

ISBN 1-85486-177-8

Create it with Thread in an Evening — In this book Caroline offers the option of applying your skills to three different mediums: quilting, appliqué and cross-stitch. All the projects are easily achievable by beginnners and great fun for all skill levels.

ISBN 1-85486-176-X

All the above titles should be obtainable from good bookshops. In the event of difficulty please contact the Books Division, Nexus Special Interests Ltd., Nexus House, Boundary Way, Hemel Hempstead, Herts HP2 7ST Tel: 01442 266551

NEW TITLE FROM NEXUS SPECIAL INTERESTS

Alice and Daisy: Edwardian rag doll sisters to make and dress
Valerie Janitch

The basic Alice & Daisy dolls are simple enough for a beginner to make and equally easy to dress, with charming colour photographs that follow Alice & Daisy through their busy social diary. Whether it's lessons, shopping, tea in the country, a birthday party or just retiring to bed, an appropriate outfit is a necessity (plus beribboned underpinnings, of course!). Be warned! Once you have made the fashion conscious rag dolls, they won't allow you to resist the temptation to make their entire wardrobe. This book gives you the instructions to make the pretty and romantic Edwardian fashions that are such an important part of their sophisticated lifestyle. Alice & Daisy may be rag dolls, but *mere* rag dolls they are not!

To be published Autumn 1998. ISBN 1-85486-183-2